Robert Cormier

WHO WROTE THAT?

Robert Cormier

Margaret O. Hyde

Foreword by
Kyle Zimmer

CHELSEA HOUSE
PUBLISHERS
A Haights Cross Communications Company ®
Philadelphia

CHELSEA HOUSE PUBLISHERS

VP, New Product Development Sally Cheney
Director of Production Kim Shinners
Creative Manager Takeshi Takahashi
Manufacturing Manager Diann Grasse

Staff for ROBERT CORMIER

Executive Editor Matt Uhler
Editorial Assistant Sarah Sharpless
Production Editor Noelle Nardone
Photo Editor Sarah Bloom
Series Designer Keith Trego
Layout 21st Century Publishing and Communications, Inc.

http://www.chelseahouse.com

A Haights Cross Communications ◀─ Company ®

First Printing

1 3 5 7 9 8 6 4 2

Library of Congress Cataloging-in-Publication Data

Hyde, Margaret O. (Margaret Oldroyd)
   Robert Cormier / Margaret O. Hyde.
      p. cm.—(Who wrote that?)
Includes bibliographical references.
   ISBN 0-7910-8232-6 (alk. paper)
   1. Cormier, Robert. 2. Authors, American—20th century—Biography.
3. Young adult fiction—Authorship. I. Title. II. Series.
PS3553.O653Z67 2004
813'.54—dc22

                                        2004022576

All links and Web addresses were checked and verified to be correct at the time
of publication. Because of the dynamic nature of the Web, some addresses
and links may have changed since publication and may no longer be valid.

Table of Contents

FOREWORD BY
KYLE ZIMMER
PRESIDENT, FIRST BOOK

HUMANITY IS POWERED by stories. From our earliest days as thinking beings, we employed every available tool to tell each other stories. We danced, drew pictures on the walls of our caves, spoke, and sang. All of this extraordinary effort was designed to entertain, recount the news of the day, explain natural occurrences—and then gradually to build religious and cultural traditions and establish the common bonds and continuity that eventually formed civilizations. Stories are the most powerful force in the universe; they are the primary element that has distinguished our evolutionary path.

Our love of the story has not diminished with time. Enormous segments of societies are devoted to the art of storytelling. Book sales in the United States alone topped $26 billion last year; movie studios spend fortunes to create and promote stories; and the news industry is more pervasive in its presence than ever before.

There is no mystery to our fascination. Great stories are magic. They can introduce us to new cultures, or remind us of the nobility and failures of our own, inspire us to greatness or scare us to death; but above all, stories provide human insight on a level that is unavailable through any other source. In fact, stories connect each of us to the rest of humanity not just in our own time, but also throughout history.

This special magic of books is the greatest treasure that we can hand down from generation to generation. In fact, that spark in a child that comes from books became the motivation for the creation of my organization, First Book, a national literacy program with a simple mission: to provide new books to the most disadvantaged children. At present, First Book has been at work in hundreds of communities for over a decade. Every year children in need receive millions of books through our organization and millions more are provided through dedicated literacy institutions across the United States and around the world. In addition, groups of people dedicate themselves tirelessly to working with children to share reading and stories in every imaginable setting from schools to the streets. Of course, this Herculean effort serves many important goals. Literacy translates to productivity and employability in life and many other valid and even essential elements. But at the heart of this movement are people who love stories, love to read, and want desperately to ensure that no one misses the wonderful possibilities that reading provides.

When thinking about the importance of books, there is an overwhelming urge to cite the literary devotion of great minds. Some have written of the magnitude of the importance of literature. Amy Lowell, an American poet, captured the concept with her statement when she said, "Books are more than books. They are the life, the very heart and core of ages past, the reason why men lived and worked and died, the essence and quintessence of their lives." Others have spoken of their personal obsession with books, as in Thomas Jefferson's simple statement: "I live for books." But more compelling, perhaps, is the almost instinctive excitement in children for books and stories.

Throughout my years at First Book, I have heard truly extraordinary stories about the power of books in the lives of children. In one case, a homeless child, who had been bounced from one location to another, later resurfaced— and the only possession that he had fought to keep was the book he was given as part of a First Book distribution months earlier. More recently, I met a child who, upon receiving the book he wanted, flashed a big smile and said, "This is my big chance!" These snapshots reveal the true power of books and stories to give hope and change lives.

As these children grow up and continue to develop their love of reading, they will owe a profound debt to those volunteers who reached out to them—a debt that they may repay by reaching out to spark the next generation of readers. But there is a greater debt owed by all of us— a debt to the storytellers, the authors, who have bound us together, inspired our leaders, fueled our civilizations, and helped us put our children to sleep with their heads full of images and ideas.

Who Wrote That? is a series of books dedicated to introducing us to a few of these incredible individuals. While we have almost always honored stories, we have not uniformly honored storytellers. In fact, some of the most important authors have toiled in complete obscurity throughout their lives or have been openly persecuted for the uncomfortable truths that they have laid before us. When confronted with the magnitude of their written work or perhaps the daily grind of our own, we can forget that writers are people. They struggle through the same daily indignities and dental appointments, and they experience the intense joy and bottomless despair that many of us do. Yet somehow they rise above it all to deliver a powerful thread that connects us all. It is a rare honor to have the opportunity that these books provide to share the lives of these extraordinary people. Enjoy.

Robert Cormier, with his unflinching, realistic look at the life of teens, revolutionized the field of young adult literature. He once said that he was an "arrested adolescent." His ability to describe the internal life of teenagers has undoubtedly made his books favorites of readers, young and old, the world over.

The Early Life of a Gentle Monster

CAN YOU IMAGINE an author deliberately tripping in front of a junior high school audience because he wanted them to see how human he was?[1] Robert Cormier (pronounced Kor-MEER) did this to show his readers that he was not the monster some felt he must be because his novels show a dark side of life. He has written about so many of the horrors teens confront that he has been accused of personally having a dark side. When his readers meet him, many are surprised to find a friendly, soft-spoken, modest, personable man. He has often been described as a sensitive man, who is not afraid to look at the dark or evil side of life and describe that side in his books. However, this does not mean that he is evil. This popular author has been called the "single most important writer in the whole history of young adult literature."[2] He is famous for writing about characters that experience many of the things he did and felt when he was growing up.

Robert Cormier was born on January 17, 1925, to a French-Canadian father and an Irish-American mother. He was the second of eight children in a close-knit family that was part of the community of Leominster, Massachusetts, a small city nestled in a valley about forty miles west of Boston. If you have read some of his books, you are familiar with Leominster under the name of Monument, the fictional town created as the setting for many of his stories.

Cormier lived in French Hill, a part of Leominster that was named for the French Canadians who moved there around the turn of the century. Frenchtown, in the book *French-town Summer*, was set in the French Hill section. French Canadians came to Leominster to work in the factories, and Cormier's grandfather was one of the immigrant workers in the town's comb factory. His grandfather accumulated enough money to buy an apartment building with three stories. This was not a luxury apartment building, but a

Did you know...

Robert Cormier lived all his life in Leominster, Massachusetts. He was born there and continued to live there with his wife until he died in 2000. He said there were lots of untold stories right there on Main Street.

tenement in which three families could live on different floors. It was one of many similar three-decker buildings that stood close together with alleys between them and small porches on each level, where tenants could enjoy sitting outside. Many of the men and women who lived there worked in the local factories all their lives. At one point Cormier's family lived on the first floor and his grand-parents lived on the third, with aunts and uncles living nearby.

Cormier's father, Lucien Cormier, worked in the comb factory in Leominster for more than forty years. He married Irma Collins, who was Irish American, and together they raised a family in Leominster. Even though he was only four years old during the Great Depression of 1929, Cormier remembered that his father had to struggle to house and feed his family at a time of extreme poverty.

When Cormier was a child, his family moved often, from one three-decker tenement house to another in French Hill. In those days, neighbors helped carry things and a borrowed truck took the place of the modern moving van. After a move, the men celebrated by sitting together and drinking homemade beer.[3]

Many of Cormier's neighbors and relatives worked with his father in the comb factory. Work in the comb factory was hard. In his novel *Fade,* Cormier describes conditions in a factory similar to one where his grandfather and father worked for many years:

> You opened the door of the Rub Room at the comb shop and a blast like purgatory struck your face. The workers sat on stools, huddled like gnomes over the whirling wheels, holding combs against the wheels to smooth away the rough spots. The room roared with sound of machinery while the foul smell of the mud soiled the air. The mud was a mixture of

Robert Cormier grew up and spent his adult life in the town of Leominster, Massachusetts, a working-class community west of Boston that is known in his books as the fictional town of Monument. He never lived farther than three miles from the house where he was born.

ashes and water in which wheels splashed so that they would not overheat at the point of contact with the combs. Because the Rub Room was located in the cellar of the shop where there were no windows, the workers toiled in the naked glare of ceiling lights that intensified everything in the room: the noise, the smells, the heat, the cursing of the men. On the coldest day of the year, the temperature in the Rub Room was oppressive; in the summer, unbearable.[4]

The Depression began when Cormier was four years old and it lasted many years. It was a time when people throughout the country felt the lack of jobs, the poverty that resulted, and the struggle to keep food on the table. While

Cormier's father, a quiet and hard-working family man, had to work at a variety of jobs in the factory during the Depression, he never complained. This added to the respect Cormier had for his father.

Robert Cormier had a close friend, Pete Dignard, who lived for a while on the second floor of the same three-decker house where the Cormiers lived. The Depression didn't bother Robert (called Bob then) and Pete much, although they knew they were poor. They had ways of making money. They scoured French Hill for empty bottles and sold them at the local drugstore for two cents each. (This was before the time of nickel refunds.) And Bob, with Pete's help, told ghost stories to the local kids wrapped in his mother's discarded bedspread. One week, he put on a circus exhibit and charged children a penny admission. Bob and Pete managed to earn enough for the Saturday afternoon movies and two-for-a-nickel ice cream cones. Like other boys, these friends played baseball, swapped baseball cards that came with bubble gum, played and swapped marbles, and rode bicycles together.

Cormier often felt that he somehow "did not belong" in school, even though his good friend, Pete, also attended St. Cecilia's Parochial Grammar School. He says he felt he was a "social disaster," but home was always a place where he felt secure. He remembers feeling threatened, when he was about twelve or thirteen, by an older boy. This boy was a bully, someone who picks on kids who are smaller and younger than himself. Cormier remembered the threat so well that he wrote a newspaper column, "Meet the Bully," years later. In it he tells about the boy who chased him through the shortcuts in his old neighborhood, even though in reality he never met the boy. The bully never caught him, and perhaps did not even want to, and he disappeared from

Cormier's life as mysteriously as he appeared. No one really knows why bullies pick on their victims, but they usually pick on quiet boys. Cormier was a rather quiet boy who was not particularly good at sports, but who enjoyed going to the library from the time he learned to read.

The dogs that chased Cormier on his paper route were not fond memories, either, but he did enjoy looking back to the hot summer nights when everyone sat on their front porches and fanned themselves with cardboard. During the heat waves, the kids were allowed to stay out late. Some nights they enjoyed eating two-for-a-nickel ice cream cones. In those days, the only flavors were vanilla, chocolate, strawberry, and occasionally butter pecan. No matter how hot the night, Cormier and his friends would run through the backyard shortcuts to the store and hurry home before the ice cream melted down the sides of the cones and onto their fingers. There was no air conditioning and not many poor people had fans. The Cormiers and their neighbors were poor, but they didn't know any rich people to compare themselves to, so they didn't mind being poor. During those heat waves, everyone shared the same problems of having difficulty sleeping at night and being uncomfortable during the day. Since schools closed early during the heat waves, the children thought of them as good times.

Even though Cormier was glad when a school day was shortened, he enjoyed reading and writing. He couldn't remember when he first wanted to be a writer; it seemed to him that it had always been his dream. In seventh grade, he had his first encouragement from someone outside of his family. A teacher, Sister Catherine, praised a poem he had written and called him a writer. This was very important to him. He remembered Sister Catherine many years later, for crediting him as a writer.[5]

One day, when Cormier was near the end of eighth grade, he looked up from his desk at St. Cecilia's School and saw that his house was on fire. He could see the flames across the street and beyond a vacant lot, and he knew his mother and baby sister were there. He wanted to rush home to make certain that they were safe, but the nun who taught the class made him say prayers first. Although his mother and sister were both safe, the nun's actions made him angry at the church for a long time. Patricia Campbell, in her biography *Presenting Robert Cormier*, describes this incident as the end of Cormier's accepting childhood and the beginning of his rebellious and questioning adolescence.[6]

After the fire, Cormier and Pete were placed with relatives or friends for a few weeks. When their families found homes, they were in different neighborhoods and the friends drifted apart.[7] Because Pete had broken a leg when they were in sixth grade, Cormier graduated from St. Cecilia's a year before Pete did. Cormier went to the junior high school, which was downtown, so he lost contact with Pete and made other friends at the new school. When kids graduated from St. Cecilia's, they entered ninth grade at a school where most had started in seventh grade. This, along with being French Canadian, made life hard for many of the kids from St. Cecilia's.

In *Fade*, Cormier has a character describe a similar situation: "We don't belong there," he said. "We'll never catch up." By this he meant that they were joining the school in the ninth grade and would be leaving by the end of the year for Monument High. "These kids have been together since the first grade. My first grade teacher called Raymond LeBlanc a Canuck. But not in a nice way. Said it like it was a dirty word."[8]

Cormier remembers his adolescence as a difficult experience, a period that he later said was not one of "peppermint fun and frolic."[9] In addition to changing schools and all the usual problems of being a teenager, he had acquired glasses. He hated his glasses, round lenses in wire frames that perched on his nose and made him the target of kids who teased him as having "four eyes." The glasses broke easily, especially when they fell off as he jumped a fence. And he hated his glasses because the stars in the movies didn't wear glasses; they were only worn by the homely, the timid, and the shy.

One time, Cormier thought of an instant cure for wearing glasses: lose them and pretend you don't need them. Although he was nearsighted, he tried living without them for a few months, saying he didn't need them any more. He had to pretend to see the blackboard and work harder to make up what he was missing. When he did not recognize his father waving to him from across the street, he had to admit that he needed his glasses.

In those years, even with the glasses, he continued to enjoy reading and going to the movies. These movies influenced his writing. For example, references to the 1933 film *The Invisible Man* are found in his book *Fade*. Cormier mentions movies in the book *I Have Words to Spend*, a collection of some of his newspaper columns. In one column called "The Days of Sweet Innocence," he lists things that the movies of his youth led viewers to believe. For instance, "the good guy always wins in the end," and "the surgeon starts each operation by saying, 'Scalpel, please.'" Moviegoers emerged from the darkened theater believing additional untruths that all librarians are spinsters, and that managing editors of newspapers always call out, "Stop the presses!"[10]

When young Robert Cormier arrived home after a Saturday afternoon movie, he would talk to his mother about it. He would tell her all the details, all the twists and turns of the plots. He would tell her scene by scene what happened. Years later he realized that this storytelling helped him on his road to becoming an author and helped his sense of story, pacing, and characterization. He subconsciously absorbed the way drama developed, and when he wrote his books, he developed them in terms of scenes, not chapter by chapter.[11]

The young Cormier, when asked what he wanted to do, always answered that his dream was to be known as a writer and to produce at least one book that would be read by people.[12] That dream came true with the publication of his first novel. He not only succeeded in writing many books, he became one of the best young adult literature authors of all time. His books encourage teens to ask more questions and look at their own lives differently. They offer pleasure to readers of all ages.

Robert Cormier always wanted to be a writer. Although he began work as many in his community did, working for the local comb factory, he got a job writing, first for radio and then for newspapers. He was able to support himself and then his family as a reporter. Only after the publication of I Am the Cheese *was he able to quit his job at the newspaper and call himself a full-time novelist.*

2

Words Wisely Spent

"I'M GOING TO write a book" is an expression heard so often that it can almost be considered a famous quote. Many people do write books, but the great majority who plan to don't even try. For those who do write them, the chance of getting their manuscripts published is slim. Most authors, including Robert Cormier, have seen many rejection slips.

Robert Cormier knew that he wanted to write from the time he was twelve years old. His mother would listen to him as he read the short stories he scribbled on scratch pads on the kitchen table. She would listen attentively and accept what he had written, not criticizing the way his teachers at school did. She would praise what he had written and she encouraged him to choose writing as his career. Cormier said, many years later, that his mother heard his stories with a sense of awe and wonder. He wrote his thanks for the encouragement she gave him in a newspaper column that became part of the collection in the book *I Have Words to Spend*.[13]

"President Cleveland, Where Are You?" is a story in his book *8 Plus 1* that has a connection to his early stories. It includes a description that came to Cormier at a time when he was scribbling stories in pencil at the kitchen table. In an introduction to the story he wrote for the book many years later, he describes his search for a description of a beautiful white house in a wealthy part of town where the girl of his dreams lived. He didn't want to describe it as a white, shining house, and he knew nothing about architecture. He read and reread what he had written, and the description finally came to him. It was "a big, white, birthday cake of a house." That old story was lost over the years, but Cormier says it was in that moment that he "discovered simile and metaphor, that words were truly tools." (A simile is a comparison of two different things using the word "like" or "as." A metaphor is a direct comparison, claiming that one thing is another.) He used the description of "a big birthday cake of a house" in the second sentence of the third paragraph of the story, "President Cleveland, Where Are You?"

Cormier continued to write stories and poetry when he went to high school. Some of his poetry was so good it was published in the local paper, the *Leominster Daily Enterprise*. He graduated from high school in 1942, at a time when the United States was fighting World War II. Many of his classmates went into the armed forces, but Cormier was rejected because his nearsightedness meant he had to wear glasses. Cormier told Jennifer Keeley, author of *Understanding I Am the Cheese*, that he was devastated by this rejection.[14] Everyone, in those days, wanted to fight the Germans and the Japanese and most of his class went in for army induction together. He tried to enlist two times later, but was still turned down.

Instead of joining the army with his classmates, Cormier went to work at a comb factory in French Hill, similar to the one in which his father worked. This was the kind of work that many people in Leominster did. He managed to work on the night shift, so he could take daytime classes at the State Teachers College at Fitchburg, a nearby town.

One of Cormier's teachers at the college, Florence Conlon, recognized his storytelling skill. Without telling him, she had one of his stories, "The Little Things That Count," typed up. She submitted it to *The Sign*, a national Catholic magazine, where it was accepted. This teacher surprised him by going to his home one Saturday afternoon and handing him the $75 check for the story, an amount that was worth more in those days than it is now. This was the first money Cormier earned for writing and was the beginning of a long and productive career.

In order to concentrate on writing, Cormier left college after the first year and took a job at a radio station, WTAG, in Worcester, Massachusetts, where he wrote radio commercials. When he applied for the job, he was asked, "What do you write?" He answered, "Just get me a typewriter, and I'll write anything you want." He later said that one could only say this at age nineteen or twenty. He did not mean to be boastful, but to express confidence.[15] Cormier had good references, including one from working in a shoe store, and he was hired as a scriptwriter for commercials. Soon after he went home, he went to the library to get some books on how to write for the radio, where you write for the ear instead of the eye. Information had to be packed into short spaces; a sponsor had a few minutes or less—sometimes only thirty seconds—for a message. This was a good lesson in discipline for a writer who had to say what needed to be said in a short time and to make the message appealing. Cormier wrote radio commercials for two years, but during that time he continued to write freelance articles. Some of these were accepted by the *Worcester Telegram and Gazette*, where, in 1948, he was hired as a reporter for the newspaper's Fitchburg Bureau.

While working at the radio station, Cormier met a girl from French Hill who had been two years behind him in high school. Her name was Constance Senay, called Connie, and she came to a community dance with his sister Gloria. After dancing with Connie a few times, Cormier knew he wanted to see more of her. They saw each other regularly for two years and were married at St. Cecilia's Church on November 16, 1948. The solid marriage, which lasted fifty-two years, played a large part in providing a safe and comfortable base for Cormier's work. Constance Cormier has been described as having a quick intelligence that was a match for her husband's brilliance.[16] Their daughter, Roberta, was born in 1951, and their son, Peter, joined them in 1953.

In 1955, Cormier took a job as a reporter for the *Fitchburg Sentinel*, a newspaper that later became the *Fitchburg-Leominster Sentinel and Enterprise*. While he was working there, his daughter Christine was born in 1957. He was promoted to wire editor of the paper in 1959. That year, his article about a child burned in an automobile accident received an award for the best human-interest story in New England from the Associated Press.

Saddened by his father's death from lung cancer, Robert Cormier began writing about his anger and grief in a story that later became his first published novel, *Now and at the Hour*. This adult novel deals with the mind of a man, a former industrial worker. He fights a battle of humiliating pain and failing health, as he comes face to face with the ordeal of his impending death. The book is dedicated to his mother and the memory of his father. Although his original title included the word death, editors convinced him to change it because they believed a title with that word would not appeal to readers. Later, Cormier wrote *After the First Death* for young adults, but by that time, he had a strong following of enthusiastic readers. *Now and at the Hour,* his first novel that was published in 1960, was praised in reviews but the sales were small.

In 1964, Cormier began writing a book review column, and five years later, he began writing a human-interest column twice weekly under the name of John Fitch IV. When it won the national K.R. Thomson Award by the syndicate that owned the *Fitchburg Sentinel* for the best human interest column, his true identity became known. Some of these columns are a major part of the book *I Have Words to Spend: Reflections of a Small-Town Editor,* assembled and edited by Cormier's wife, Constance, and published in 1991. In the same year that Cormier received the K.R. Thomson Award, he was honored by The New England Press Association for the best news story under pressure of deadline.

Cormier said he was a novelist disguised as a newspaper-man for thirty years.[17] Thus it is not surprising that, in addition to his newspaper work, Cormier wrote fiction on weekends and at night. He called this his dessert. He would rather write than play golf, and he spent many hours at the

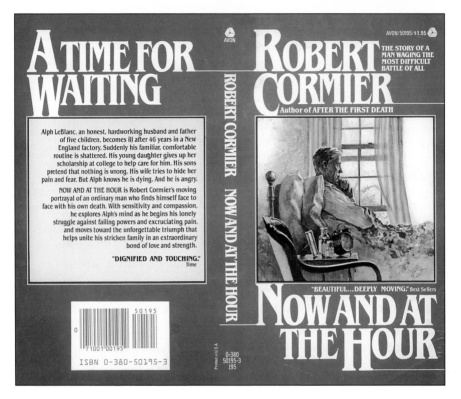

THE STORY OF A MAN WAGING THE MOST DIFFICULT BATTLE OF ALL

Author of AFTER THE FIRST DEATH

Alph LeBlanc, an honest, hardworking husband and father of five children, becomes ill after 46 years in a New England factory. Suddenly his familiar, comfortable routine is shattered. His young daughter gives up her scholarship at college to help care for him. His sons pretend that nothing is wrong. His wife tries to hide her pain and fear. But Alph knows he is dying. And he is angry.

NOW AND AT THE HOUR is Robert Cormier's moving portrayal of an ordinary man who finds himself face to face with his own death. With sensitivity and compassion, he explores Alph's mind as he begins his lonely struggle against failing powers and excruciating pain, and moves toward the unforgettable triumph that helps unite his stricken family in an extraordinary bond of love and strength.

"DIGNIFIED AND TOUCHING."
Time

"BEAUTIFUL...DEEPLY MOVING." Best Sellers

Robert Cormier's first published novel, Now and at the Hour, *was inspired by his father's battle against lung cancer. Although sales of the book were modest, it won critical acclaim.*

typewriter after his day at the newspaper office. He would get home early and be there when his kids got home from school. He would take a nap late in the afternoon or right after dinner. In the evenings, when things quieted down, he would write, often between the hours of 10:30 P.M. and 1:00 A.M. This meant he was always awake when the kids came in from their dates or movies. They provided a lot of material for his writing. Even when the kids were home, he never shooed them away while he was writing. He never worked in a room with a door, but in an alcove off the dining room, a place that was separated only by an archway.

Cormier describes his children's teenage years in an introduction to his stories that made up the book *8 Plus 1*:

> The house sang in those days with the vibrant sounds of youth—tender, hectic, tragic, ecstatic. Hearts were broken on Sunday afternoon and repaired by the following Thursday evening, but how desperate it all was in the interim. The telephone never stopped ringing, the shower seemed to be constantly running, the Beatles became a presence in our lives.[18]

Cormier wrote many short stories in those years when his children were growing up. Some of his short stories were published by *The Sign*, the Catholic magazine that bought the story he wrote while at Fitchburg State College; *The Saturday Evening Post*; *Redbook*; *Woman's Day*; and *McCall's*. The money from these stories helped to support his growing family. In 1967, Cormier's fourth child, Renee, was born.

Short story writing was not Robert Cormier's favorite form of writing, but it helped pay for his family's expenses. These stories have been described as warm and gentle, hardly a description of his later novels for young adults. In both short stories and novels, however, he drew on his experiences as a child and adolescent in French Hill.

In the years Cormier worked on the newspaper, he said he thought of himself as a novelist. After his first published novel, the one inspired by his father's death, he wrote two more novels for adults. *A Little Raw on Monday Mornings* and *Take Me Where the Good Times Are* were both critically acclaimed but did not cause much of a stir. *Take Me Where the Good Times Are* is the book in which he established the fictional setting of Monument, the small New England town modeled after his home town of Leominster and the location in which he set much of his later fiction. Shortly after, Cormier finished two other novels that were never published.

The Chocolate War, the novel that followed these two unpublished works, created a stir. Cormier sent the manuscript to his agent, Marilyn Marlow, to place the story with a publisher as another adult novel, but she said that it sounded like a Young Adult novel, one meant for readers between the ages of twelve and eighteen. Cormier had not written the book with this market in mind. The first two chapters of *The Chocolate War* included some language that might be too strong for teens, and the story moved fast and had complex symbolism. However, Cormier feared that making it suitable for young readers would tame the story and it would lose its true meaning. The first editor who read it appreciated the story but felt it was too depressing for young people. So did the next few editors who read the manuscript.

One editor offered to publish the story and give the author an advance of $5,000 if he would change the ending. Although this offer was tempting, Cormier refused to make the ending happy. He claimed, "A happy ending attached to

Did you know...

Robert Cormier was not surprised that his books made him a target for censors. Since the opposite of love is indifference, not hate, he said that he hoped readers would not find they had a feeling of indifference when they read his novels.

a novel whose flow and tone and development is downbeat fatally flaws the work."[19] He believed that an ending should be true and believable, not like television shows in which you know the problems will be solved at the last minute and the ending will be happy. Kids know this is a phony view of life.

Eventually, Cormier's agent found a publisher who would accept the story as written. The publication of *The Chocolate War* was an important step in the world of young adult literature. The book, which was published in 1974, was an instant success. Robert Cormier had found his audience. This and the young adult novels that followed made Cormier popular with teenagers around the world. He changed the entire landscape of teen books. According to noted critic and writer, Michael Cart, "He is, simply, the single most important writer in the field that is made distinguished by his contributions to it."[20]

Cormier, the founding father of teenage fiction, is considered one of the best American writers in the past fifty years.[21] Today, people of all ages read and enjoy Cormier's words and will continue to do so for years to come.

In this movie version of The Chocolate War *(1988), Jerry (Ilan Michael-Smith) is bullied by Archie (Wallace Langham) into selling boxes of chocolates for the school's annual fund-raising event.*

3

Do I Dare Disturb the Universe?

ROBERT CORMIER BEGINS *The Chocolate War*, perhaps his most well-known book, with this single sentence, "They murdered him." It describes a boy who was trying out for the football team, and his "murder" was the beating he took from the team. The book isn't about real murder, but many of Cormier's books are as intense and as exciting as murder mysteries. They deal with the real lives of young people. Cormier has been credited with being a groundbreaker in terms of writing novels that expose real-life, difficult issues for teens.[22]

He writes about the achingly awful world that exists for many teens but that had, for the most part, been glossed over by most writers of books for young adults. In his books, there are no happy endings, no parents ready to lend a helping hand. Cormier has admitted that he writes to upset and to provoke the reader. He has said that he knows how an adolescent feels because he is an arrested adolescent, and that today's adolescents feel the way he felt when he was younger. Times have changed, clothing and music are different, but the emotions, the longings, and the doubts are changeless.[23]

The Chocolate War began as an event in the lives of the Cormier family and grew from the author's imagination about what could happen when a boy is told to sell chocolate candy for a fund-raising event. When a child brings boxes of candy home to sell for a school fundraiser, his family probably groans. Usually such fundraisers mean pestering the neighbors, nearby relatives, and friends to buy as many boxes as they will. Some students talk their family into buying the whole batch so they won't put the neighbors and friends in an awkward position. When Cormier's family was confronted with what to do about selling chocolates for a fundraiser at the Catholic school attended by their son, Peter, they discussed the problem at the dinner table. After the discussion, Peter decided on a different choice: Take the candy back to school and politely refuse to sell it.

Cormier told his son that his refusal would not appear on his report card; there would be no "CHOCOLATE SALE: FAILURE" in with his grades. His father even wrote a note saying he supported Peter's decision about the chocolates. So the next day, Cormier drove Peter to school and watched him as he carried the two bags of candy up the walk.

Notre Dame High School, in Leominster, Massachusetts, is the real-life high school that Robert Cormier's son attended. Peter's refusal to sell chocolates as a school fund-raiser proved to be the inspiration for The Chocolate War. *It all began with Cormier asking the question, "What if?"*

Peter took the chocolates back to school, gave them and the letter to the headmaster, and that was the end of the story. Before Robert Cormier knew the real ending of the story, however, he wondered what would happen when his son returned the chocolates. What if the other students gave him a hard time? Would the headmaster of the school hold it against him? What if he was the only one in the school who didn't sell at least a few of the boxes?[24]

"What if?" was a typical way of thinking for Robert Cormier. His "what if" was the basis for many of his novels.

In this case, it was the beginning of *The Chocolate War*, in which a main character, Jerry Renault, refuses to sell chocolates for the fundraiser.

Jerry, stunned by his mother's death and upset by the way his father walks sleepily through life, is a very real character. He attends Trinity, a private Catholic school for boys in which the acting headmaster, Brother Leon, is a cruel, sadistic man. Leon has bought 20,000 boxes of chocolates to sell as a fundraiser, and he desperately needs them sold in order to repay the cost of the candy and to make money for the school.

Jerry's refusal to sell chocolates is based on an order from the school's secret society, the Vigils, who play an important part in the school's everyday life. Archie Costello, leader of the Vigils, gives out assignments to new students and random victims. No one refuses an assignment for fear of making life worse. Jerry was ordered to refuse to sell the chocolates for ten days, but, on his own, Jerry continues to refuse. At first, other students see him as a hero, but Archie Costello changes that and makes Jerry's life miserable.

Archie is a nasty, ill-behaved person who is hated by the students, but most of all he is feared, and for this reason he can manipulate them. Archie is manipulated himself by the evil Brother Leon. Leon uses Archie and his power over the Vigils to make certain all the chocolates are sold. Archie is such a powerful leader that the students are afraid to support Jerry in his stand against evil. Because of his stance, Jerry lives in a world of abuse of power and gang rule, where his locker is trashed and his phone rings all hours of the day and night but the callers do not talk. Even his homework is stolen. Jerry becomes an outcast.

Jerry is not sure why he continues to refuse to sell the chocolates, although perhaps he was influenced by the poster in his locker that read: DO I DARE DISTURB THE UNIVERSE? He did not refuse to sell the chocolates because he consciously dared to disturb the universe, but his action disturbed the small universe of his school. He stands against the abuse of power by Archie and the acting headmaster until the sad ending, where he is physically beaten. At that point, he says that he should have just gone along with the system. "They tell you to do your thing, but they don't mean it. They don't want you to do your thing unless it happens to be their thing, too. . . . Don't disturb the universe. . . . Otherwise they murder you."[25]

Teen readers flocked to the book and continue to do so. They read it first and foremost because it is a good story. Robert Cormier says he was not trying to send a moral

Did you know...

The New York Times Book Review described *The Chocolate War* as masterfully structured and rich in theme (Summer Reading List, *New York Times Book Review*, 1974).

This book made publishing history with its uncompromising portrayal of the manipulation of people and the misuse of power. Jerry Renault, the main character in the book, has been compared with Martin Luther King, Jr., who led a mass struggle for racial equality. Brother Leon's classroom has been seen as a metaphor for Nazi Germany.

message, but to write a believable story with believable characters. A closer look at the story reveals that while the hero sticks to his principles, no one comes to his rescue. There is an implicit lesson that bad things happen when good people do nothing. The wrong people win and the right people suffer. Whether or not readers find this in the sad ending, *The Chocolate War* has been called the book that persuaded commentators to take the literary tastes of young adults seriously.[26]

In 1974, when *The Chocolate War* was published, reviewers of young adult literature were used to happy endings. Between 1930 and 1960, young adult books depicted children in happy families, where the girls and boys had few emotional problems. There was adventure in the books, and there were issues about popularity and dating, but good triumphed over evil. By the end of the 1960s, characters in young adult novels had more serious problems than the early novels. They dealt with abuse, suicide, and drugs, but still, by and large, the endings were upbeat.

With the sad ending of *The Chocolate War,* Robert Cormier dared to disturb the universe. There were good reviews of *The Chocolate War*, soon after it was published, but some of the reviews in magazines important to librarians, the librarians who order books for high-school and public libraries, were very much against the book. One review, which appeared in the American Library Association's *Booklist* on June 1, 1974, had a heavy black border, somewhat like a funeral notice. The heading was "Whammo, You Lose," and the book was described as having see-through characters and a powerfully stacked plot. Cormier was accused of manipulating readers into believing how rotten things are.[27]

A review appearing in England claimed *The Chocolate War* presented the worst aspects of American life in a neat package.[28] Many reviewers, both in England and America, had negative things to say about the book, but other reviewers praised it. For example, Theodore Weesner wrote in the *New York Times* that the book was masterfully structured and rich in theme and that complex ideas unfolded with clarity. He suggested it as an ideal study for the high school classroom. As it turned out, this was a good prediction. *The Chocolate War* has been translated into more than a dozen languages, and it is taught in hundreds of schools and in adolescent literature courses in colleges and universities.[29] It is now considered classic literature.

Amid all the controversy of the reviewers about *The Chocolate War*, many young adult readers expressed their opinions. They understood the emotions and the experiences of the characters in the book. They appreciated the honesty of the book, one in which the good guys don't win. They were, and continue to be, strong supporters of Robert Cormier.

One story about the controversy created by *The Chocolate War* involves students who were assigned to read the book before entering ninth grade at a school in Groton, Massachusetts. Some parents and some members of the school committee were so concerned by the book that they convened a town meeting to discuss the problem. Nearly 150 people came to argue whether or not this book and others with similar material should be kept out of the hands of the students.

Some reviewers criticized the book for having "an abundance of violence and disruption coupled with veiled references to less than wholesome sexual activities." Two students replied to this criticism by writing a letter in which they pointed out that a high school student does not have to open a book to read worse things than those found in *The Chocolate War*. "A trip to a restroom will expose us to far more obscene material." After much discussion, most of the school board and the parents in the audience of the town meeting supported keeping the book in the classroom.[30]

When Robert Cormier visited the school in Groton, he learned that students who were in the class that caused this controversy had circulated a petition in support of the book. When one student suggested that everyone in the class sign the petition, another student pointed out that following pressure to sign the petition would show that they did not understand the message of the book, which supports the right to stand against the system.

In addition to being read and studied in many English classes, the book is sometimes used as a springboard to discuss other subjects. For example, in studying *The Chocolate War*, students are often asked to compare Brother Leon's classroom to Nazi Germany. Both Brother Leon and Hitler inspired support and obedience through fear. Both the students at Trinity and the majority of people in Germany remained silent in the face of evil.

The book continues to inspire both admiration and controversy. According to Robert Foerstel's book, *Banned in USA*, *The Chocolate War* ranked fifth on a list of books most frequently banned in American public libraries and schools in the 1990s. At the same time, it regularly appears on lists of best books, including the *School Library Journal's* list of "The Best of the Best 1966–1978."

Cormier's portrayal of good versus evil is common in many of his books other than *The Chocolate War*. He realized that kids want reality and know that the good characters don't always win in life. Robert Cormier's books reach beyond the happy endings of television, where problems are often quickly solved. His heroes are often tragic, suffering from the power of pressure to conform. He frequently considers the subject of the individual versus the system, and his extraordinary insight into the world of adolescents provides powerful messages that continue to disturb the universe.

The actor Robert Wagner played Dr. Brint, a psychologist probing into the mysteries of Adam Farmer's shadowy past, in a 1983 movie adaptation of I Am the Cheese. *Makers of the movie, unlike the author of the book, felt compelled to add on a happy ending.*

4

I Am the Cheese

WHAT HAPPENED AFTER *The Chocolate War*? If you read the book, you are probably among the many people who want to know more about what happened to Jerry after he was left in a puddle of his blood on the floor of the boxing ring at Trinity School. What happened to the evil Archie and the other characters? Robert Cormier would write *Beyond the Chocolate War*, but not until he had written several other successful books.

His next book, *I Am the Cheese*, may have started because Cormier read a newspaper article about the witness protection program, in which witnesses against powerful criminals are given new identifies to protect them from the criminals. They have new homes, new names, and new backgrounds, so they will not be recognized. What would this do to a teenager? Cormier had written a short piece about a boy riding a bicycle one Wednesday morning. Later, he asked himself why the boy was not in school. Where was he going and why? Suddenly, he thought of the boy as part of the witness protection program. He had an idea for a plot in which the leading character is a boy who suffers from the fear of being followed.

In the book the boy on the bicycle is Adam Farmer, pedaling his old-fashioned bike mile after mile, trying to reach his father. Adam knows his own name, but that is about all he knows about himself. Who is he? Where was the rest of his life? In this book about Adam's search for identity, Cormier keeps the suspense alive through brilliant craftsmanship. Readers don't know what is happening, since they are only given one clue at a time. The boy's journey becomes the readers' own journey as they travel along with the boy on the bike in some chapters of the book and read transcripts of what appear to be Adam's therapy sessions in other chapters.

Chapters about adventures on the bike ride and the transcripts of the therapy sessions are skillfully interwoven. Adam tells his story in the present tense. The reader assumes the transcript material is taking place in the present tense; but later in the book the transcripts reveal information about Adam and his family in the past tense. The author uses these techniques to maintain the suspense that the reader feels building throughout the book, as the narrative jumps back and forth between the boy's quest and the tapes.[31]

Adam is a shy teenager who would rather hang out with books and records than play with other kids. He is an outsider by choice, one who has difficulty in sharing his private life with others, even with Amy, the character in the book who is his friend and first love. From time to time, as he rides along on his bike, he considers calling Amy. When he does try to call her, a strange man answers the phone, leading Adam to think that Amy has moved away.

The number given in the book that Adam used to call Amy was Cormier's actual home phone, and information spread quickly that Robert Cormier would answer the phone when readers would call. If a caller said she was Amy, Cormier would go along the idea. A typical caller would ask if he were Dad. Then Cormier would fill the role of Amy's dad, perhaps asking if she was in trouble. Cormier might ask if Adam was with her, and the conversation would continue as if they were real characters in the book. In a talk given in 1987, Cormier said he got at least one call a day after the book was published.[32] Some of the callers became lifelong friends.[33] Sometimes these calls came after the author had spoken to a group at a high school. No matter where they originated, Cormier played the game. He said that it was a tribute to young people that he never had an obscene call, or wise-guy call, or middle-of-the-night call during the many years after the book was published. And it is a tribute to Cormier, who made himself available to young readers for so many years.

Young readers of *I Am the Cheese* are fond of Adam, who represents an individual fighting against the system. They relate easily to the shy and confused teenager, who is struggling to find clues of his former life. Sometimes while Adam is riding his bike, he remembers singing the children's nursery rhyme "The Farmer in the Dell" with his parents in the front seat of a car. He sings snippets of it now and then as he pedals along, and the song comforts him. The song was the Farmer family's theme song, and Adam drifts in and out in his search for reality. He never sings as far as the last lines of the "Farmer in the Dell," in which the rat gets the cheese, and the cheese stands alone. Only at the end of the book does Adam know that he is the cheese.

When Adam pedals his bike on the long, long trip toward his father, he carries a package that is precious to him, and the reader wonders what is in the package. The content of the package is a mystery, a part of the suspense that holds the reader's attention for page after page. At the end of the book, when the content of the package is revealed, the reader is confronted with the extent of Adam's confusion and the truth at its root. In one review, the secret that is the root of Adam's identity is described as exploding like an H-bomb.[34]

When *I Am the Cheese* was published, adult critics admired Cormier's literary workmanship and highly sophisticated style. Some were again concerned that the book might be too complex for teen readers. In *I Am the Cheese*, Cormier broke three rules of young adult fiction. The first is that, as in *The Chocolate War*, there is an unhappy ending. Cormier wants the reader to feel the high emotion that Adam experienced. How could Adam, who is so fearful and locked in an institution, come up with an escape plan? Cormier is willing to sacrifice the happy ending to make his characters real.[35] The second rule that Cormier broke is avoiding a political message. *I Am the Cheese* shows the murky world of a corrupt government, one with a relationship to organized crime. Cormier definitely breaks the third rule, that a young adult book must be simple and straightforward, in *I Am the Cheese*. While some critics found the complexity of the book irritating, others praised it for not being another run-of-the-mill book for teenagers. It was described as a serious and challenging book of great merit.[36]

Some young readers, however, found the book complex and difficult to understand. One young reviewer thought that the story line was lost in trying to create a vivid picture and that the book has a weak ending. Others called it a fantastic novel. Several young readers wrote reviews of the book in which they said the way pieces were fit together was pure genius. One reader called it a fantastic book with a twisted ending. Many young adult readers gave the book high praise and said they appreciated having an introduction to psychological thrillers. Many identified with Adam's fears, such as fears of closed spaces, of dogs, and about who can be trusted, and identified with Adam's questioning of his identity and his feeling of isolation from others. Adam's searching for self has been called an exaggerated version of the identify crisis of the teen years.[37]

The publication of *The Chocolate War* and *I Am the Cheese* led to significant changes in the life of the Cormier family. Before the books' publication, Cormier had held his daytime job as a newspaperman and written novels at night and during other "non-working hours." With the success of these two young adult novels, he became a full-time writer. The decision to give up his regular paycheck did not come easily, since he was a child of the Depression. But his wife persuaded him to write full time, and as a result, the world of young adult literature became greatly enriched.

Did you know...

I Am the Cheese is a psychological thriller. "It is a sophisticated novel of psychological suspense." The secret revealed at the end struck some readers as an explosion of an H-bomb. Robert Cormier appeared in the film version of *I Am the Cheese*.

(Quote from the Outstanding Books of the Year, *New York Times Book Review*, 1977.)

The title of the book After the First Death *is taken from a poem by the Welsh poet Dylan Thomas. The last line of the poem reads, "After the first death, there is no other." Cormier enjoyed reading poetry and prose throughout his life. He used phrases from some of his favorite poems as titles for his books—for example,* Tunes for Bears to Dance To *(from Gustav Flaubert's novel* Madame Bovary*) and* The Rag and Bone Shop *(from William Butler Yeats's poem "The Circus Animals' Desertion").*

5

After the First Death and the Margaret A. Edwards Award

SUPPOSE A PARENT were to use the absolute trust of a son or daughter for his own ends. This is one of the thoughts that led Robert Cormier to write *After the First Death*. His own twelve-year-old daughter, Renee, greatly admired and completely trusted him. But what if he betrayed her trust? Cormier envisioned such a father as a character in one of his forthcoming books. Cormier had also considered having a character in a novel who was a "California girl," someone who was blonde and beautiful and seemed to have a perfect life. And a third character, who brought the story together, grew out of the story of innocent children being killed by a bomb thrown into a post office. Cormier asked himself, "What kind of person could do that?" He lived fifteen miles from the Fort Devens army base, and one day, while driving by it, he wondered what went on there. Were there secrets valuable to terrorists hidden there? All this thinking came together in *After the First Death. Newsweek* magazine described the book, published in 1979, as a marvelous story written in crackling prose that deals not only with topical issues of terrorism, but abuses of power, loyalty, betrayal, courage, and fear.[38]

Cormier initially thought *After the First Death* might become the love story that he had always wanted to write. Instead, it became a complex and controversial suspense novel told from multiple points of view. Three main characters, Ben, Miro, and Kate, meet for the first time on a bridge on a hot summer day after a busload of children has been hijacked by terrorists seeking the return of their homeland. Before the hijacking is described, one narrative is told by Ben, the son of the general who is in charge of the forces whose task is to release the hostages. Ben tells of his part in the operation and his relationship with his father. Two other narratives are given, one by Miro and one by Kate. Miro is a young terrorist for whom this experience of killing a person for the first time is to be a rite of passage. The reader learns about this assignment, about some of Miro's conscious fears, and about some of his training. The reader will not condone his attitude but will get some understanding of his motivations. He is supposed to kill Kate, the sixteen-year-old girl who is the substitute bus driver.

In the book, Kate tells about her past, how she tries to stay alive in the bus, how she helps the children, and how she tries to escape the terrorists. She is an important character in the book, and the only one who shows true courage. When Cormier was asked why Kate died in the book, he said that Kate was an amateur pitted against professionals and that amateurs often commit errors. Then he added that he did not kill Kate, Miro did.

Perhaps the book's most tragic character is Ben, whose father makes him a pawn for the sake of patriotism. Cormier provides clues throughout the book and attempts to tie the various threads of the story together at the end of the book.

The book's title, *After the First Death*, is taken from a poem by Dylan Thomas called "A Refusal to Mourn the Death, by Fire, of a Child in London." The last line of the poem reads, "After the first death, there is no other." Although many of the characters in the book appear to die more than once, Patricia Campbell, a friend and authority on Robert Cormier, quotes Cormier in an interview as saying that the first death is so devastating that others pale beside it.[39] In this complex novel, some of the characters die first a moral and emotional death, and then a literal death. *After the First Death* demands work on the part of the reader. Sometimes what appears to be real may not be;

Did you know...

Robert Cormier loved jazz, movies, and staying up late. He also loved reading and writing. His writing has left us with literature that will continue to be read for many years by both young adults and adults.

what you are being told by characters may or may not be true. Even the ending is open to interpretations. Yet this terrorist thriller has been read and reread by adults as well as young adults the world over, and many consider it the best book they have ever read. Not everyone applauded the book when it was published, however. One reviewer wrote that she was appalled at the author's abuse of his considerable power to involve impressionable young readers.[40] In spite of some negative criticism when it was published, *After the First Death* was one of the three books that earned Robert Cormier the important Margaret A. Edwards Award in 1991. This book, along with *The Chocolate War* and *I Am the Cheese*, was described as a brilliantly crafted and troubling novel that achieved the status of a classic in young adult literature. The award honors an author whose work has been taken to heart by young adults over a period of years, "providing an authentic voice that continues to illuminate their experiences and emotions giving insight into their lives."[41]

The Margaret A. Edwards Award is presented soon after the recipients are chosen and they must be present to receive it. Therefore the authors are contacted immediately after they are chosen. One author had to be contacted by ship-to-shore radio because he was traveling in the Panama Canal Zone. Another author was away celebrating the birth of a grandchild. When Robert Cormier was called, he was appropriately at home reading a library book.[42]

In accepting the award, Robert Cormier said that he was delighted to be the recipient because it is was such a clear reflection of what he had always hoped his novels would do—show adolescents the bigness of what's out there and that happy endings are not our birthright. He added, "You have to do something to make them happen."[43]

The field of young adult literature—literature written for and marketed to young adults—was still young when Robert Cormier received the Margaret Edwards Award, but it had grown. It had matured from straight adventure and the romantic fluff that characterized many books in the first half of the twentieth century to books with realistic characters, important themes, and fine writing. Robert Cormier's work certainly filled these descriptions. Today, he is well known as a thought-provoking author of some of the finest young adult fiction.

British author H.G. Wells's novel, The Invisible Man, *shown here in the 1933 movie featuring Claude Rains, was an inspiration for Cormier's novel* Fade. *Wells told the story of a man who discovered a way to make himself invisible. The author Stephen King has said, "Imagine what might happen if Holden Caulfield stepped into H.G. Wells's* Invisible Man, *and you'll have an idea how good* Fade *is." Holden Caulfield is the hero of J.D. Salinger's* Catcher in the Rye, *a novel that, like many of Robert Cormier's books, still appears on banned book lists.*

6

Teens Want More Robert Cormier

TEENS ENJOY READING novels that tell them the truth, so it is not surprising that Robert Cormier's writing was and continues to be welcomed by young readers. His books tell of problems young people face every day and the emotions they experience with an extraordinary insight into the adolescent world. His novels encourage teen readers to ask more questions and look at their own lives differently. His books recognize the evil in the world and don't include happy endings to please readers who want them.

Cormier's first three young adult novels explore the dark corners of the mind and make readers examine their own feelings and beliefs. But the dark side of the mind that made the first three young adult novels so exciting was missing in Cormier's next book, published in 1980. Titled *8 Plus 1*, the book is a collection of stories that were written in the ten years between 1965 and 1975. Some of these stories had appeared in magazines such as *The Saturday Evening Post* and *Redbook*. In later years, some of the stories appeared in collections of short stories and school textbooks.

Many of Cormier's young adult readers were disappointed by these stories, which seemed to be written by a middle-aged author for an audience of the same age. The main characters in four of the stories are fathers, making them less interesting for teens looking for characters their own age; however, the stories are warm, tender, and very personal.

One reviewer wrote that in *8 Plus 1* we see a gentler Cormier, not one who is writing about evil and the starkly realistic parts of life. One feature that makes the book different from others is an introduction to each of the stories that gives some information about how it was written or some of its background. This book may have interested young people desiring to become authors, but most young readers preferred the page-turning suspense of Cormier's other books.

Robert Cormier's next book, *The Bumblebee Flies Anyway*, was a great success. John Knowles, in the *New York Times Book Review*, called it eloquently written and affecting, and many readers found the novel unforgettable. It is set among terminally ill teens who are in an experimental medical institution. Sixteen-year-old Barney

Snow is a victim of memory experiments and suffers from amnesia (loss of memory). He has only fleeting memories of his past life, and some of them include flashes of driving a red convertible. Barney knows that he is different from his friends, the terminally ill patients who live at the institution with him, because he does not appear to be terminally ill. He bonds with the other patients as he tries to help them. One character, Mazzo, who is dying from cancer, has a twin sister, Cassie. She visits the clinic and brings a taste of the real world with her. Barney develops a friendship with Cassie, who has the strange characteristic of feeling her twin brother's pain. She wonders what will happen to her when he dies.

The Bumblebee Flies Anyway is an eerie, suspenseful tale that raises haunting questions about identity, but it is also a story of hope, courage, and friendship. The title of the book is taken from the old myth that a bumblebee's body is too big for the size of its wings, so it should not be able to fly, according to the laws of aerodynamics. The idea that the bumblebee flies, even though it is not supposed to be able to do so, is often cited as an example of something that defies conventional wisdom and expectations. So it was with Barney. Even though he was an experimental subject in a clinic, he showed others that he could "manage to fly."

Barney helps his friends deal with their problems. He builds a mock up of the red car that he has fleeting memories of driving in his past. In his nightmares, he feels that he is about to crash in the car. Using parts from the junkyard that is near the hospital, Barney and his friends assemble a car they call the Bumblebee. When it is finished, in a dramatic gesture of faith and hope, the group sends the Bumblebee soaring out of an attic window. Even though this novel takes place in a hospital for the terminally ill, it is considered one of the author's most affirmative novels. According to J.B. Cheaney, who interviewed Robert Cormier, Barney Snow's ultimate response to death suggests the Christian doctrine of resurrection.[44]

Robert Cormier's next book, *Beyond the Chocolate War*, was published in 1985, two years after *The Bumblebee Flies Anyway*. This book was the only sequel he ever wrote. Patricia Campbell tells us in *Presenting Robert Cormier* that the author wrote and discarded hundreds of pages for this manuscript, enough to fill a huge cardboard box.[45] When the book was published, a reviewer for the Children's Book Review Service described it as a brilliant sequel, more finely crafted, denser in plotting, and more subtle in nuance than at his debut ten years ago as a young adult author.[46]

Did you know...

Robert Cormier's books have been translated into more than a dozen languages, including German, French, Italian, Swedish, Chinese, and Japanese. His books have been reprinted many times, and one (*Heroes*) is in large print for readers with vision problems. Many have been recorded on tape, and three, *The Chocolate War*, *I Am the Cheese*, and *The Bumblebee Flies Anyway*, have been made into movies.

Archie Costello, the devious leader of the Vigils in *The Chocolate War*, continues to command the Vigils, the school's secret society, handing out troublesome assignments to meek students. But Obie, Archie's important helper, is drifting away from him. In a story of friendship, relationships, loneliness, anger, jealousy, and guilt, Cormier makes the reader feel as if he or she were there in Monument, attending secret meetings of the Vigils.

This dark, suspenseful, and riveting book is a great read. Robert Cormier created a sequel that many readers liked as well, if not better, than the original. This is often not the case for sequels. In this book, as in many others, Cormier showed his unique ability to integrate personal, moral, and political themes.

The author Stephen King has praised Cormier's next book, *Fade*, as his best novel. "Imagine what might happen if Holden Caulfield stepped into H.G. Wells's *Invisible Man*," King said, "and you'll have an idea how good *Fade* is."[47]

Have you ever wondered what life might be like if you were able to become invisible? In *Fade*, a novel that includes three stories set in three decades, the secret gift/curse of becoming invisible is passed from one person in each generation to someone in the next. In 1938, in the small town of Monument, Massachusetts, thirteen-year-old Paul Moreaux discovers that he can "fade."

When Paul first discovered his ability, he was aware that something was very different. He says:

I was in the pause again, caught in that strange place between darkness and the light, my breath taken away, panic racing along my flesh. And the flash of pain, as if my body were a taut wire through which bolts of electricity passed, unendingly, excruciatingly. At the point where I gathered myself to scream, the pain fled, the pause ended, air filled my lungs and the cold vanished. I was suddenly whole again, restored, intact, visible, here and now—Paul Moreaux, in the second-floor tenement of my grandfather's house on Eighth Street. Everything the same as before. But not really the same again. Never to be the same again.[48]

Paul's uncle, who also has the ability, attempts to teach him about the phenomenon. At first Paul is thrilled with this strange ability, but he finds what appears to be a gift can be a curse. Paul's actions make him scary both to the reader and to himself.

The next part of the story is told from the point of view of an editor reading a manuscript thirty years later. It was the story Paul wrote about himself after he became a recluse and famous writer. The third part is Paul's story of his search for the person in the next generation who is able to fade. Paul discovers this boy and finds that he has been abused and is deeply disturbed. He is less able to handle the fade than those who had it before him and has great capacity for doing evil things.

Robert Cormier said in an interview that the writing of *Fade* was a labor of love, and the most autobiographical he had ever done.[49] Both he and Paul Moreaux were thirteen in 1938 and both grew up in the French-Canadian part of a town in Massachusetts similar to Monument. *Fade* is a gripping story in which Cormier deals with dark subjects with compassion and grace. He explores issues of morality and power, and feelings of isolation and depression, as he does in most of his novels. In this book, as in others, the author leaves his readers with a sense that the story has not ended. This is one of the characteristics that make his books so suspenseful.

The teens and many other readers who composed Robert Cormier's readership continued to want more great books by the author—and to their pleasure, he continued to write them.

Robert Cormier at an autographing session. He not only spent time with his fans, he also spoke at school boards and conferences defending the right of young adults to read and have access to his controversial books.

7

Other Bells for Us to Ring . . .

OTHER BELLS FOR US TO RING, published in 1990, is a different book from the dark novels that preceded it, although it is a sad story. It was written for a somewhat younger audience than the earlier books. *Other Bells for Us to Ring* is a novel about a young girl, Darcy, growing up during World War II. Darcy feels isolated when her father is transferred to an army camp in Massachusetts in Monument, the same town in which most of Cormier's other novels take place. She doesn't know anyone her age, but she soon makes friends with a vivacious girl, Kathleen Mary O'Hara, who exposes Darcy to the Catholic faith. Darcy is both terrified and fascinated with the Catholic rituals that Kathleen Mary interprets for her.

After Darcy learns that her father is missing in action, she endures another blow. Her friend, Kathleen Mary, suddenly disappears. Darcy's mother suffers from migraine headaches and is little comfort to her. Darcy has a crisis of faith that she attempts to resolve with a secret visit to an elderly nun she has seen helping others. The nun explains the beauty of life and faith to her and helps her deal with her problems. At the end of the story, Darcy's father is found to be safe, but Kathleen Mary's story is sad, for she dies after she moves away. According to a review in the magazine *Publishers Weekly, Other Bells for Us to Ring* is beautifully written, but it raises many more issues about God, miracles, growing up, and alcoholism than it resolves.[50]

Robert Cormier returned to the dark side of novels that made him famous in *We All Fall Down*, a book published in 1991. It was the love story he had wanted to write, but it does not have the usual happy ending of most love stories. Cormier said he was apprehensive about writing it because he was not sure if he could reach young people in a love story using his own instincts. But after the book was published, he had some wonderful letters from readers, including one who wished that the ending could be happy, but she knew it could not.

We All Fall Down opens with a shocking scene that pulls the reader into the story.

They entered the house at 9:02 P.M. on the evening of April Fools' Day. . . . At 9:51 P.M., the invaders left the house, abandoning the place as suddenly as they had arrived, slamming the doors, rattling the windows, sending shudders along the walls and ceilings. They left behind twenty-three beer cans, two empty vodka bottles and damage later estimated at twenty thousand dollars, and, worst of all, Karen Jerome, bruised and broken where she lay sprawled on the cellar floor.[51]

Karen's sister, Jane, is badly affected by this tragedy, which leaves Karen hospitalized in a coma. Jane no longer relates to friends the way she used to, and she becomes a loner. Buddy, one of the boys who trashed the house, secretly watches Jane over a period of time, feeling guilty because of the trouble he has caused. Buddy has trouble at home because of his parents' divorce and he develops a problem with alcohol. Jane meets Buddy after he trips and falls, while in the process of spying, and soon after they fall in love. This complex novel is written from several points of view. One is from a character called the Avenger, who sees all that it going on and whose goal it is to exact revenge for the trashing. The characters come together at the end of the book.

Cormier makes you feel sympathy for even the worst characters, and in this book, he once more deals with themes of good and evil. While reviewers called the book compelling, powerful, and richly textured, some readers did not like it. Many thought it was a great book, and some found that even though tragic feelings were set up, the book ended on a feeling of hope.[52]

The same year that *We All Fall Down* appeared in print, Cormier published a collection of his newspaper columns and stories. This book, *I Have Words to Spend: Reflections of a Small Town Editor*, was assembled and edited by his wife, Constance. It consists of eighty-five stories that Cormier originally wrote as newspaper columns and short stories that he wrote when he was a journalist. Many of these stories were written in the evenings after work.

There are childhood memories, nature stories, short pieces about favorite movies, travels, and family experiences, and more. Many readers enjoy keeping this well-written book where they can pick it up from time to time and read something entertaining about the details of everyday life.

Next came *Tunes for Bears to Dance To*, a book, like *Other Bells for Us to Ring*, that was written for younger readers. Once more, the author writes about goodness and evil, and the abuse of power. The story concerns eleven-year-old Henry, whose older brother has been killed by a hit-and-run driver and whose family has just moved to different town. His father is so depressed after the brother's death that he cannot work, and his mother works long hours as a waitress trying to earn enough

Did you know...

Robert Cormier enjoyed reading poetry and chose some of the titles for his books from his favorite poems. These poems range from the nursery rhyme "The Farmer in the Dell" (*I Am the Cheese*) to the sophisticated work of Gustav Flaubert (*Tunes for Bears to Dance To*) and William Butler Yeats (*The Rag and Bone Shop*).

money to keep the family together. Henry works, too. His boss is a grocer, Mr. Hariston, a mean-spirited man who enjoys being nasty to Henry.

Henry notices a man who walks by each day on his way to a rehabilitation center. When Henry meets the man, Mr. Levine, he learns that he is a survivor of a Nazi concentration camp. Henry and Mr. Levine become friends, and Mr. Levine shows Henry the village he is carving at the town craft center. It is a replica of his village that was destroyed during the Holocaust in World War II.

Henry is unaware of his employer's bigotry and tells him about his friendship with Mr. Levine. One of Henry's ambitions is to buy a monument for his brother's grave. Mr. Hariston promises Henry that he will buy the monument, see that his mother gets a raise, and let Henry keep his job at the grocery store if he will do one easy task. That task is destroying the carved village that Mr. Levine has made. Does Henry hurt his new friend or help his family survive? Readers, like Henry, are confronted with how they would behave in the face of evil.

The book is a masterful portrayal of manipulation, survival, and prejudice. Some readers wish they could know more about Henry and his family at the end, but it is typical of a Cormier book to leave the reader wanting to know more.

Some readers have asked what the title, *Tunes for Bears to Dance To*, has to do with the book. Some expected to find dancing bears in the story. The title is taken from a quote by the French writer Gustav Flaubert: "Human language is like a cracked kettle on which we beat out tunes for bears to dance to, when all the time we are longing to move the stars to pity."[53] In this quote from *Madame Bovary*, Flaubert refers to the inadequacy of language to express our feelings. What we hope for often falls short of the reality of life.

Cormier's next book, *In the Middle of the Night*, was published in 1995. The book began with Cormier's thinking back to a terrible fire at Boston's Coconut Grove nightclub in 1942, where 490 people were killed. Once more he asked himself, "What if?" and he imagined a catastrophe in a movie theater. Suppose that a young usher was blamed for starting a fire that led to the collapse of a balcony, crushing the children under it. Cormier built a many-layered story around this idea.

When he was sixteen years old, Denny Colbert had no idea about the life-changing experience of his father, John Paul. All he knew was that the phone in his house rang often at night and his parents told him never to answer it. He didn't know that his father had worked as an usher in a theater where there had been a horrible accident. John Paul had been sent to the balcony to check on some noises. He didn't have his flashlight, so he lit a match in order to see better. Just as he dropped the match and the matchbox, the balcony collapsed, killing twenty-two children and severely injuring others. For years after the accident, which was wrongly blamed on John Paul, he received hate letters and phone calls in the middle of the night accusing him of the accident. John Paul's sense of guilt affects his family, especially Denny, who wishes he could live the kind of life other teens live.

Denny's life changes when he disobeys his parents and gives in to his urge to pick up the phone. He becomes involved with one of the handicapped children, Lulu, who is seeking revenge against his father.

In this typical Cormier book, the emotions of hatred, revenge, and guilt are explored and the ending is not a happy one. The novel features a fast-moving plot, well-developed characters, and a surprise ending. One young reader wrote, "If you read only one book in your whole entire life, you must read this one."[54]

Robert Cormier when he received an honorary doctorate from Fitchburg State College. Although he attended the school for only one year as a student, Cormier had a long and significant history with Fitchburg State. His writing career began when one of his professors at Fitchburg sent his short story to The Sign, *a national Catholic magazine. Cormier's papers are also housed in the college library.*

8

Tenderness, Heroes, Frenchtown Summer, and *The Rag and Bone Shop*

MANY TEENS AND adults have looked forward to each new Cormier book from the time they have read their first one. After *The Chocolate War* in 1974, there was a new novel every year or two. Beginning in 1997, a Cormier book was published each year until his death in 2000. His last book, one that was finished just before he died, was published a year later. When asked which book they like best, many of his avid readers have a hard time deciding.

Rereading a Cormier novel is often even more enjoyable than the first read. Just as this author hated to finish writing a novel because he grew attached to the characters and loved to rewrite to make them better, his readers ponder on his novels long after they have set them down. Many find the second reading an even better experience than the first, for they uncover more of the wealth of meanings, themes, and emotions in Cormier books. And although reading each novel is a distinct experience, there are many themes, such as identity, intimidation, loss of innocence, guilt, and forgiveness that run through the books. Some of these many themes can be found in *Tenderness*, a book published in 1997.

Tenderness is another of Cormier's books that began with the idea "What if?" Cormier had been reading articles about the justice system's practice of keeping a young person charged with a crime in a juvenile detention facility until he or she reaches the age of eighteen. Then, no matter what the crime, the offender is released into society. What if a boy who had committed murder was free to commit another murder when he was released? Suppose he met a girl who yearned for tenderness and fell in love with him, not knowing that he would continue to be a murderer? Cormier combined these characters in a story about the idea that feelings of tenderness can also carry pain.

Did you know...

Robert Cormier usually spent about a year and a half writing each novel, although *The Bumblebee Flies Anyway* took five years. He wrote the complete story of a book and then he rewrote it until he found the perfect word or phrase. He is famous for his brilliant use of simile and metaphor and as a master of suspense. His novels look dark on the surface, but they always contain moral values at their core.

The quotes that open the book mention two kinds of tenderness: "A part of the body that is injured and tender to the touch," and "To know the pain of too much tenderness."[55] The latter is a line from a book by the famous poet Kahlil Gibran, who wrote *The Prophet*. Patty Campbell tells of a remark made by Cormier in an interview about the novel. He said that that line had haunted him for years.

Tenderness is the story of Eric, an eighteen-year-old boy who was released from juvenile detention after killing his mother, his stepfather, and two other teens. Eric doesn't feel emotion the way most people do. He is a warped and dangerous person. Still, he longs for someone to be tender with him, a tenderness he finds in caressing and killing beautiful girls. Lori is a naïve young girl who has run away from a bad home situation. She sees Eric's picture on the television screen while she is in a diner. The news that he is being released from juvenile detention is far less important to her than recognizing him as a boy who once treated her kindly. Lori arranges to meet Eric, an act that becomes her undoing.

Tenderness is written from the point of view of three people: Lori, Eric, and Jake. Jake is a retired detective who is obsessed with bringing Eric to justice for his crimes. He thinks of Eric as a monster and stalks him over a period of time in both legal and illegal ways. While he is watching Eric's actions, he hears about Lori and thinks she could be the key to catching Eric.

Cormier writes in a way that makes readers feel they are in the minds of the characters. He is even able to build up sympathy for the convicted killer. If you read about Eric and his crimes in a newspaper article, you would not feel the same about him as you do if you read the book. When Eric cries in his cell at the end of the book, many readers will feel concern and empathy for him. While many reviewers were disturbed because of the sympathetic portrayal of Eric, Patty Campbell, an authority on Robert Cormier, has described it as one of his most popular books.[56] Some say it is Cormier at his best.

Heroes, Cormier's next book, explores the nature of heroism. Cormier's heroes are people who do their duty, day after day. For example, he considered his father, who labored year after year to support his family, a hero. The idea for the book came about the time of the fiftieth anniversary of D-Day, June 6, 1944, when Allied troops in World War II invaded the German-held coast of France. Obituaries of local men and women who died in the invasion were republished in Cormier's newspaper, along with the records of many of the brave things that ordinary people did in the war. These people and their actions motivated Cormier to write *Heroes*.

Published in 1998, *Heroes* is a tender, tragic portrait of Francis Joseph Cassavant. In this gripping coming-of-age story, Francis, the main character of the story, served in World War II. He returns home after the war with his face badly damaged. Although Francis is seen by others as a hero, he is not certain that he really was one. He deliberately fell on the grenade that destroyed his face. Although this action saved many lives and he received the Silver Star for his heroic effort, Francis knows he was really trying to commit suicide out of guilt and shame over actions committed before the war.

When Francis returns home, he keeps his identity secret. He walks the streets of Frenchtown, the French-Canadian part of the town of Monument, remembering the old days before he went to war and waiting for the return of Larry LaSalle, his former friend. Through flashbacks, the reader comes to know Larry as the person who helped Francis to overcome his shyness as a teen. Larry was a popular leader and he even helped Francis win the love of a beautiful girl named Nicole.

Before Francis and Larry went to war, however, an episode occurred in which Larry raped Nicole, while Francis was hiding nearby. Although Francis blames himself for not saving Nicole, he now seeks revenge for what Larry did. What happens when they meet and how the situation is resolved is an exciting part of the book.

Many parents did not think that young people should be reading about the many-sided ethical issues of rape, suicide, and murder. Some demanded that *Heroes* be removed from school reading lists. Once again, a Cormier book was being censored.[57] But more than one teacher felt that this book helped young people deal with these issues. Many teens and adults alike find *Heroes* to be so exciting they hate to put it down. The characters remain with them, as if they were alive.

In *Frenchtown Summer*, published in 1999, Cormier surprised many of his fans by using poetry to look back on his twelfth summer, telling a semi-autobiographical story about a boy named Eugene, who is searching for his identity. The form of the poetry is called lyrical free verse, which is unrhymed verse with no restrictions regarding its metrical structure. It received much critical acclaim, and one reviewer refers to as an "exquisite novel."[58] The book is not the dark story that one finds in many Cormier novels, but one that is shadowed with mystery. Each chapter is an episode, leaving the reader with much to ponder.

Eugene spends the hot summer of post-World War I in Frenchtown. He is a lonely, observant boy who gets his first pair of glasses, falls in love with a nun who visits Monument to teach piano, stands by a friend who experiences a medical condition called St. Vitus's dance, connects his uncle to an unsolved murder, and learns still other secrets of Frenchtown. What he wants to learn most is if his silent and withdrawn father really loves him, and he finds this out in an unusual way. All the activity happens in the fictional town of Monument, with the landmarks familiar to readers of other Cormier books: the tenements, the alleys, the streets, the Catholic Church, the comb factories, and the shops.[59]

Cormier described his use of free verse in *Frenchtown Summer* in this way: "I was thinking in terms of a long short story. But it kept falling into these rhythms. So I thought, why not go along with them?"[60] A *Christian Science Monitor* review of the book notes that the lyrical verse gives the story an unexpected degree of warmth and tenderness.[61] The book is especially enjoyable when heard on audiocassette.[62]

Robert Cormier's next book was a gift to his church. He said that his Catholicism had always been a boon and a burden. When he was young, the nuns taught him to behave for fear of punishment. They told him that thoughts of girls were evil.[63] But when he was older, Cormier found his religion a comfort and experienced a renewed appreciation of the enduring values that it taught him. Many of his books have a theme of an individual's response to evil, and they are often described as delivering powerful moral statements. Cormier wrote a history of his parish, *Portrait of a Parish*, as a gift to St. Cecilia's Church, where he had worshiped all his life, before writing his last novel, *The Rag and Bone Shop*.

The title of *The Rag and Bone Shop* is taken from a poem, "The Circus Animals' Desertion," by Irish poet William Butler Yeats. Yeats is considered one of the greatest English-language poets of the twentieth century. Robert Cormier chose this title for a novel in which he describes Trent, a policeman, who is an expert in getting people to confess. Trent says he listens to the foul things that people do to each other. He describes himself as one who must

> . . . lie down where all the ladders start,
> In the foul rag and bone shop of the heart."[64]

Those lines from Yeats's poem had been his credo through the years. Trent had some sleepless nights from listening to the crimes and from forcing people to confess. But he was good at what he did.

The book is set, once more, in Monument, Massachusetts, where seven-year-old Alicia Bartlett has been battered to death. The last person who saw her alive was Jason, a shy twelve-year-old boy who spent hours talking to Alicia and doing jigsaw puzzles with her. He seems an unlikely friend because he is so much older than she is. He also seems an unlikely murderer, but there are no other leads and Jason has no alibi. Trent is pressured to get a confession by politicians, and his high-powered questioning of Jason is the major part of the novel. Trent holds a perfect record for getting confessions, and he plays mind games with Jason. When Cormier writes that the game of cat and mouse is over, he alludes to the line from Yeats's poem that gives the book its title: "We now go down to where the ladders start."[65] This reminds the reader that sometimes, to get to the truth, they must go to a place they would call the pits ("the foul rag and bone shop of the heart").

Young Jason, who is intimidated by the questioning, has no clue as to what is going on. Trent twists Jason's mind so that the boy finds himself questioning what is really true. Trent manages to wring a confession from Jason, even though he knows Jason is innocent. Trent, who has his own emotional problems, feels shattered after it is revealed that Jason is not the murderer.

The book is a brilliant character study written as a terrific chiller. The shocking ending stays with the book's readers long after they have finished the story.

*Cormier, a young fan, and Dr. Marilyn McCaffrey, the former guardian of the
Robert E. Cormier Collection at Fitchburg State College in Massachusetts.
The young woman is reading from* After the First Death, *one of the three books
that earned Cormier the important Margaret A. Edwards Award in 1991.
The Robert E. Cormier Collection includes correspondence, drafts of his
writing, reviews, fan letters, and a section on the censorship of his work, and
will help scholars researching the life and work of this important author.*

9

Robert Cormier: A Hotline to the Hearts and Minds of Teens

A BOOK BY Robert Cormier is an invitation to walk with his characters through their personal lives, especially through their tragedies. When Cormier wrote, he was very conscious of his readers. He said in an interview that he was an "arrested adolescent."[66] Certainly, his books showed that he understood the hearts and minds of teens. He remembered from his own youth how a fourteen-year-old boy or girl feels about him- or herself and about life. The loneliness and the sense of being an outsider he experienced as a bookish child are portrayed in many of his books. Although he did not write his first book for young adults until he was in his late forties, he believed the longings and the doubts that young adults have are time-less. Such things as styles of clothing and music change, but the emotions experienced as teens grow up remain the same. People feel many of these same emotions no matter how old they are.

Many adults, even teachers, feel they can protect children by having them read only stories with happy endings, with people who step in to lend a helping hand and act as role models. They think children will be safe from the harsh realities of life if they read only about life's good things. Robert Cormier felt that dealing with tragic events, and trying to portray life more realistically, would help children handle some of the difficult problems they might encounter later in life. Living though dark times with the characters in a book can give readers strength when they confront problems in their own lives.

Nonetheless, Cormier's grim realism resulted in the censorship of some of his books. This censorship usually consisted of attempts to keep his books from being avail-able in the library or being taught in classes. On this issue, Cormier has said that parents have a right to decide what their children should read, but that censorship controls what other children read as well, and this is not fair.

In addition to writing, visiting libraries, and speaking to groups of children, teens, and adults, Cormier spent some of his time fighting censorship of his books. Three of his books, *The Chocolate War*, *We All Fall Down*, and *Fade*, made the list of 100 Most Frequently Challenged Books of 1990–2000. He defended his books at town debates, at school board meetings, and in interviews. He felt that many adults think children live in a vacuum and are unaware of their exposure to the darker side of life in television, movies, and even what happens at school and on school buses. Few children grow up without exposure to the realities of good and evil, no matter how carefully their books are screened. There are some who already live with serious problems. Cormier had a talent for writing about life's problems from the perspective of a young person.

Free discussion of Cormier's darker books in schools gives teachers a chance to discuss complex issues and gives students a chance to say what they like and what they don't like, without fear of censorship. It's this freedom that Cormier supported. His subjects offer a wide variety of topics for debate. The good person doesn't always wear the white hat, and the evil one isn't always easily recognized as such. People don't always act to stop cruelty when they see it. Parents aren't always perfect role models, and they are notably absent or unimportant in many young people's lives. Cormier told the truth, and while these truths made his books a target for censors, it also helped to make his books extremely popular with young adults.

When asked how he was able to write for young people, Cormier often said that he did not sit down at his typewriter with the idea that his readers would be young adults. He wrote for the intelligent reader and that reader often turned out to be fourteen years old. Although he did not write for adolescent readers in particular, he was careful about his choice of words. He felt that it wasn't so much the subject matter that was important but how the subject was handled. For example, in his book *Tenderness* one character is a young girl whose face is young and childlike, but her body is mature and womanlike. Rather than speak of her large breasts, he talked about her top. He said it would have been easy to write more explicit material, but he held himself to certain standards. The hard part was to suggest and contain those suggestions.

Most readers say they read Cormier's books because they enjoy them. Producing a good story was a major reason for writing his books, but Cormier said that he also wrote to provoke his readers. He didn't try to protect or coddle them, and believed that the truth could be a warning for what may happen to young people when they grow up.

Many of Cormier's readers are already grown. Some are adults who reread the Cormier books they enjoyed many years ago, and some are adults who are reading his books for the first time. Some are reading Cormier's books again now that their own children are reading them. Some readers are adults who want to be writers and are studying the style and technique of a very successful writer.

Robert Cormier was often asked to give advice to people who want to write a book. His skill as a writer is widely accepted, even by his harshest critics. He grabs the reader's attention right at the beginning of a book with an event or a character's powerful emotion and makes his readers care about his characters, and never lets the readers lose interest. Cormier creates incidents and conflicts between people, and he uses many small climaxes to hold the reader's attention. His prose style has been called brilliant. He uses a rhythmic flow of words, writing and rewriting until he is satisfied with what he has written. Many writers check what they have written one time. After Cormier wrote something, he went over the material again and again, changing words and phrases until he found just the right ones. Many people dislike this part of writing, but Cormier said he loved doing this. He said that a brain surgeon had to get it right the first time, but authors can write and rewrite many times.[67]

Cormier suggested that writers, before they write, should read many kinds of books. He said that reading is practice for writing, much as playing ball is practice for playing a game. Then he suggested setting up a daily schedule and writing something every day. A writer needs the discipline of working whether or not he or she feels in the mood. Even Cormier says he would probably only write three times a year if he only wrote when he felt like it.[68]

Cormier had his favorite authors, some that he read and reread. He considered the books of the English writer Graham Greene as the ones that taught him most, and said that he tried to write as well as Greene did (although he did not actually try to imitate him). Cormier said that when he read and reread Graham Greene's novel, *The End of the Affair*, it made him feel like writing.[69] He also turned to J.D. Salinger's short stories. Many young people are familiar with Salinger's *Catcher in the Rye*. Cormier cites Thomas Wolfe, Ernest Hemingway, and John O'Hara as being among his favorite authors. Robert Cormier enjoyed reading detective stories, noting that

Did you know...

One of Robert Cormier's editors said that Cormier explained that Ernest Hemingway had inspired him because he discovered that Hemingway did not need to use fancy three- or four-syllable words to be a great writer. (Quoted by A. Waller Hastings, Northern State University, Aberdeen, South Dakota.)

they always delivered a beginning, middle, and satisfying climax.[70]

Robert Cormier said he started his stories with an emotion, something that happened that affected him. He did not make outlines for his books, although he had a sense of where they were going. He found excitement in creating characters, and he experienced great joy in writing. He said the whole process was a never-ending source of delight.

Robert Cormier's books have been a delight to readers around the world and continue to be popular with students, teachers, and those who have read them in the past. Perhaps you know of a Robert Cormier Fan Club. It is not uncommon for a librarian who is asked about Cormier's books to respond, "Oh! I love him."

A collection of Robert Cormier's work and material connected with it is housed in Fitchburg State College Library in Fitchburg, Massachusetts. This collection includes a wide range of material. One group includes his published works, drafts of his writing, editorial correspondence, and miscellaneous items. A second group contains materials about Robert Cormier and his work, including reviews of his writing, criticisms, bibliographies and interviews, awards and honors, and more.

In the second group, there is an interesting censorship section containing articles from newspapers that document attempts of school boards to have Cormier's books withdrawn from libraries and from teachers' reading lists. It includes the author's ideas about censorship, correspondence between the author and various groups of teachers and librarians, and articles and pamphlets about book censorship that he had collected.

There are folders for each of his novels that contain fan letters only. One especially interesting article in the collection is the bicycle used in the movie version of *I Am the Cheese*. There is a tremendous wealth of other material.

Robert Cormier died on November 6, 2000, at the age of seventy-five. People who had the privilege of knowing Robert Cormier say he was a wonderful man. Readers who know him only through his books would agree.

1 Campbell, Patricia J. *Presenting Robert Cormier*, Boston, MA: Twayne Publishers, p. 9.

2 Hastings, Wally. English 240—Literature for Younger Readers, Robert Cormier (1925–2000). *http://www.northern.edu/hastingw/cormier.html.*

3 Cormier, Robert. *I Have Words to Spend*, New York: Delacorte Press, 1991, pp. 23–24.

4 Cormier, Robert. *Fade,* New York: Delacorte Press, 1998, p. 64.

5 Teenreads.com, Author Profile: Robert Cormier, "Past Interview," April 21, 2000. *http://www.teenreads.com/authors/au-cormier-robert.asp.*

6 Campbell, Patricia J. *Presenting Robert Cormier*, p. 14.

7 Cormier, Robert. *I Have Words to Spend*, pp. 21–23.

8 Cormier, Robert. *Fade,* pp. 105–106.

9 Authors and Artists, Vol. 3, pp. 65–76.

10 Cormier, Robert. *I Have Words to Spend*, pp. 177–178.

11 Hearne, Betsy, ed. *The Zena Sutherland Lectures, 1983–1992,* New York: Clarion Books, 1993, p. 102.

12 *http://www.randomhouse.com/kids/author/results_spotlight.*

13 Cormier, Robert. *I Have Words to Spend*, p. 92.

14 Keeley, Jennifer. *Understanding I Am the Cheese,* San Diego, CA: Lucent Books, 2001, pp. 17–18.

15 ACHUKA.com, Robert Cormier interview, London, July 2000. *http://www.achuka.co.uk./special/cormier02.htm.*

16 Campbell, Patricia J. *Presenting Robert Cormier*, p.16.

17 "Sample Books Ideas for Literature-Based reading Enthusiasts, *We All Fall Down* by Robert Cormier." *http://www.ucalgary.ca/~dkbrown/yrca_cormier.html.*

18 Cormier, Robert. *8 Plus 1,* New York: Pantheon, 1980, page vii.

19 Campbell, Patricia J. *Presenting Robert Cormier,"* p. 56.

20 Cormier, Robert. *http:www.randomhouse.com/kids/author/cormier/html.*

21 Thorn, Michael. "Robert Cormier," *The Scotsman,* March 19, 2001.

22 Obituary, "Robert Cormier, of Leominster, 75, Renowned Author, " *Boston Herald,* November 3, 2000.

23 ACHUKA.com, "Robert Cormier Meets Melvin Burgess," *http://www.achuka.co.uk/special/cormburg.htm.*

24 Cheaney, J.B. "Teen Wars: The Young Adult Fiction of Robert Cormier," *The World and I*, December 1, 2001. *http://www.highbeam.com/library/doc3.asp?DOCID =1...*

25 Cormier, Robert. *The Chocolate War*, New York: Pantheon Books, Random House, 1974, p. 248.

26 "The Chocolate War: Critical Overview," The Chocolate War Pass, *http://www.enotes.com/chocolate-war/9067/print*.

27 Hearne, Betsy. "Whammo, You Lose," *Booklist*, 1974, p.1199.

28 Campbell, Patricia J. *Presenting Robert Cormier*, p. 46.

29 "Robert Cormier, November 2, 2000." *http:/www.murrieta.k12.ca.us/alta/library/cormier*.

30 Campbell, Patricia J. *Presenting Robert Cormier*, pp. 48–49.

31 Keeley, Jennifer. *Understanding I Am the Cheese*, p. 74.

32 Hearne, Betsey. *The Zena Sutherland Lectures, 1983–1992*, pp. 95–96.

33 Cheaney, J.B. "Teen Wars: The Young Adult Fiction of Robert Cormier," *The World and I*, December 1, 2001.

34 *Publisher's Weekly*, March 7, 1977, cited in Keeley, Jennifer. *Understanding* I Am the Cheese, p. 85.

35 Keeley, Jennifer. *Understanding I Am the Cheese*, p. 34.

36 Keeley, Jennifer. *Understanding I Am the Cheese*, p. 36.

37 Review, "I Am the Cheese." *http://www.twinlakes.k12.in.us/schools/rms/LitWeb/cheese.html*.

38 Thomson, Sarah L. *Robert Cormier*, New York, Rosen Publishing Group, 2003, p. 55, quoted in Tony Schwartz, "Teen-ages' Laureate," *Newsweek*, July 16, 1979, p. 87.

39 Campbell, Patricia J. *Presenting Robert Cormier*," p. 77.

40 Educational Paperback Association, "EPA's Top 100 Authors, Robert Cormier." *http://www.edupaperback.org/showauth.cfm?authid=80*.

41 American Library Association, "Margaret A. Edwards Award, 1991 Winner Robert Cormier, Award Citation. *http://www.ala.org/ala/yalsa/booklistsawards/margaretaedwards/maeprevious/1991awardwinner.htm*.

42 Ibid.

43 Author, *http://www.kidsread.com/authors/au-cormier-robert.asp*.

44 "Teen Wars: The Young Adult Fiction of Robert Cormier." *http://www.highbeam.com/library/doc3.asp?DOCID +1...*

45 Silvey, Anita. "An Interview with Robert Cormier," *Horn Book*, March /April 1985, quoted in Campbell, *Presenting Robert Cormier*, p. 137.

46 Quoted in Amazon.com, Editorial reviews, *Beyond the Chocolate War*. *http://www .amazon.com/exec/obidos/ ASIN/044090580X/ 102-6660329-8948161.*

47 Cormier, Robert. *Fade*, New York: Delacorte Press, 1988, book jacket.

48 Cormier, Robert. *Fade*, N.Y.: Bantam Doubleday Dell Publishing Group, p. 73.

49 Kidspace at the Internet Public Library, "Robert Cormier." *http://ipl.si.umich.edu/div/kid space/askauthor/Cormier.html.*

50 *Other Bells for Us to Ring*, Publishers Weekly, November 16, 1990, *http://www.highbeam.com/ library/doc3.asp?DOCID =1G1:9113322&num=1.*

51 Cormier, Robert. *We All Fall Down*, New York: Delacorte, 1991, pp. 1 and 3.

52 Quoted in Amazon.com, Editorial reviews, *We All Fall Down*. *http://www.amazon.com/ exec/obidos/tg/detail/-/0440215560/ qid=1084908535/sr=1-2/ref=.*

53 Pelton, Jessica. "Do We Dare?" LiteratureClassics.com (2001). *http://www.literatureclassics.co m/essays/363.*

54 Laraway, J. "This book is a must read!" Amazon.com Editorial reviews, *In the Middle of the Night. http://www.amazon. com/exec/obidos/ASIN/ 0440226864/qid=1094821933/ sr=ka-1/ref=pd_ka_1/ 103-1324874-4941444.*

55 Cormier, Robert. *Tenderness*, New York: Delacorte Press, 1996, p. 1.

56 Campbell, Patty. "A Loving Farewell to Robert Cormier," *The Horn Book Magazine*, March 1, 2001.

57 The American Library Association, "The 100 Most Frequently Challenged Books of 1990–2001." *http://www.ala .org/ala/oif/bannedbooksweek/ bbwlinks/100mostfrequently .htm.*

58 Greever, Ellen. "Young Adult Books in Review," The Alan Review, Digital Library and Archives, Winter 2001.

59 Campbell, Patty. "Review of *Frenchtown Summer*," *The Horn Book*, September 1, 1999.

60 Thorn, Michael. "Robert Cormier," Obituary, *The Scotsman*, March 10, 2001, *http://www.highbeam.com/ library/doc3.asp?DOCID =1...*

61 Review of *Frenchtown Summer*, *Christian Science Monitor*, February 2, 2000.

62 Cormier, Robert. *Frenchtown Summer*, 2 cassettes, New York: Random House Listening Library, 2000.

63 Thorn, Michael. "Robert Cormier," Obituary, *The Scotsman*, March 10, 2001

64 Cormier, Robert. *The Rag and Bone Shop*, New York: Delacorte Press, 2001, p. 71.

65 Ibid, p. 123.

66 ACHUKA.com, "Robert Cormier Meets Melvin Burgess," *http://www.achuka.co.uk/ special/cormburg.htm*.

68 Hoffman, Laura B. "Conversations: Beyond the Shadows of Robert Cormier," Writes of Passage, USA, 1996, *http://www.writes .org/conversations/conver_4 .html*.

67 Ibid.

69 Kidspace at the Internet Public Library, "Robert Cormier." *http://ipl.si.umich.edu/div/ kidspace/askauthor/Cormier .html*.

70 Ibid.

1925 **January 17** Robert Edmund Cormier was born in Leominster, Massachusetts.

1939 Graduated from St. Cecilia's Parochial School.

1942 Graduated from Leominster High School.

1943 Enrolled at Fitchburg State College after being rejected by the Army.

1944 First story, "The Little Things That Count," published in *The Sign*, a Catholic magazine.

1946 Began work at radio station WTAG, in Worcester, Massachusetts, writing commercials.

1948 Married Constance Senay. Began working as a reporter for *Worcester Telegram and Gazette*.

1951 Daughter Roberta was born.

1953 Son Peter was born.

1955 Became a reporter for the *Fitchburg Sentinel*.

1956 Daughter Christine was born.

1957 Award for Best Human Interest Story of the Year, The New England Associated Press. Promoted to wire editor, *Fitchburg Sentinel*.

1960 *Now and at the Hour* published.

1963 *A Little Raw on Monday Morning* published.

1965 *Take Me Where the Good Times Are* published.

1966 Promoted to Associate Editor of *Fitchburg Sentinel*.

1967 Daughter Renee was born.

1969 Began writing a human interest column for the *Fitchburg Sentinel* under the pseudonym John Fitch IV.

1973 Awarded best human interest story of the year by The New England Associated Press for the second time.

1974 *The Chocolate War* published. K.R. Thompson Newspapers award for best column.

1977 *I Am the Cheese* published. Left *Fitchburg Sentinel* to write full time. Honorary Doctor of Letters, Fitchburg State College.

1979 *After the First Death* published.

1980 *8 Plus 1* published.

1981 Robert Cormier Collection established at Fitchburg State College.

1983 *The Bumblebee Flies Anyway* published.

1985 *Beyond the Chocolate War* published.

1988 *Fade* published.

1990 *Other Bells for Us to Ring* published.

1991 *We All Fall Down* and *I Have Words to Spend* published.

1992 *Tunes for Bears to Dance To* published.

1995 *In the Middle of the Night* published.

1997 *Tenderness* published.

1998 *Heroes* published.

1999 *Frenchtown Summer* published.

2000 *Portrait of a Parish* published.

2001 Cormier died on November 6, 2000. *The Rag and the Bone Shop* published.

THE CHOCOLATE WAR

Jerry Renault, who attends a Catholic high school in New England, is asked to sell chocolates for a fundraiser. His defiance is a threat to the school and causes a showdown that turns him from hero, to outcast, and finally to victim. Jerry has a sign in his locker that reads, "Dare I Disturb the Universe?" This book disturbed the whole world of young adult literature. Jerry stood alone, fighting the whole school, in a novel that is gripping and powerful.

I AM THE CHEESE

In this thriller, Adam rides his bike on a search for his father, who he believes in staying at a hospital. Adam is actually searching for his own identity after his life becomes filled with lies and deception. He has many adventures as he tries to uncover his past in this tale of government corruption, espionage, and counter-espionage. Taped sessions of Adam and his therapist help to weave Adam's mysterious past with the present. Clues given throughout the book are woven together at the end of this suspenseful story.

FADE

Paul Moreaux was thirteen when he learned about his ability to fade, or make himself invisible. When he is in the fade, he learns some shocking secrets that drive him to commit a chilling act. Paul learns that the gift is passed along from uncle to nephew and discovers that the recipient of the fade in the next generation is a damaged, vicious boy. There is a climatic showdown between Paul and his uncle.

1960 *Now and at the Hour*

1963 *A Little Raw on Monday Mornings*

1965 *Take Me Where the Good Times Are*

1974 *The Chocolate War*

1977 *I Am the Cheese*

1979 *After the First Death*

1980 *8 Plus 1*

1983 *The Bumblebee Flies Anyway*

1985 *Beyond the Chocolate War*

1988 *Fade*

1990 *Other Bells for Us to Ring*

1991 *I Have Words to Spend* and *We All Fall Down*

1992 *Tunes for Bears to Dance To*

1995 *In the Middle of the Night*

1997 *Tenderness*

1998 *Heroes*

1999 *Frenchtown Summer*

2000 *Portrait of a Parish*

2001 *The Rag and the Bone Shop*

ADAM FARMER

In *I Am the Cheese*, Adam rides his bicycle pedaling along the road to Vermont to find his father. He is on medication and has suffered from the loss of his parents as well as a change in identity. He is confused about who he is, who he has been, and what his future will bring.

There is a concrete reason for Adam not knowing his identity. His identity changed when his parents joined the government's witness protection program. After his father testified against organized crime, the whole family was given a new identity in order to protect them. Adam is alienated from every one around him, although he does remember snatches of the song, "Farmer in the Dell." His father used this song to help the family adapt to their new name, Farmer.

Adam remembers his girlfriend, Amy, and the games they played together. He shared his dreams of becoming a writer with her, but he can no longer reach her when he calls her on the phone. Adam has sessions with a therapist, who is trying to unlock secrets he believes Adam knows, while pretending to help him find himself.

When Adam finally sings the whole song of the Farmer in the Dell, including the last line—"The rat gets the cheese, and the cheese stands alone"—he knows he is the cheese.

ARCHIE COSTELLO

Archie is one of the cruelest characters in any of Cormier's books. In *The Chocolate War*, he is leader of the Vigils, a secret society in his high school, where he controls the assignments given to new students. Some of these assignments are much like gang initiation rites. One assignment, given to Jerry Renault, is to refuse to sell chocolates for the school fundraiser. Archie manipulates a teacher named Brother Leon, other students, and even the entire student body. Archie has the ability to recognize what will really hurt a person. He uses the Vigils for his own advantage or just for fun, and he manages to do this without receiving punishment himself.

PAUL MOREAUX

When the main character of *Fade*, Paul Moreaux, turned thirteen, he discovered he could make himself invisible, or "fade." He inherited this ability from his uncle, and he will pass it on to another generation. Paul is bewildered when he first experiences this power of invisibility, but he soon learns that his gift shows him some shocking secrets. After he uses the fade to murder a man who has abused his aunt and had his father attacked, he fears the power of the fade. He separates himself from society and lives like a hermit. He writes the story of his experiences with the fade, and this manuscript is discovered and read at a later date. Still later, a second part of the manuscript is found. In it, Paul gives an account of his search for the next "fader." He discovers this nephew and finds he is a deeply disturbed boy. Paul writes about how he deals with him.

Amazon.com. See material under individual titles.

Bagnell, Norma. "Realism: How Realistic Is It? A Look at *The Chocolate War*." *Top of the News*. Winter, 1980, p. 214.

Barnesandnoble.com: See material under individual titles.

Campbell, Patricia, J. "A Loving Farewell to Robert Cormier." *Horn Book*. March 1, 2001.

Campbell, Patricia, J. *Presenting Robert Cormier*. Boston: Twayne Publishers, 1985.

Campbell, Patricia, J. Review of *Frenchtown Summer. Horn Book*. September 1, 1999.

Foerstel, Herbert. *Banned in USA: A Reference Guide to Book Censorship in School and Public Libraries*. Westport, CT: Greenwood Press, 1994.

Hearne, Betsy. *The Zena Sutherland Lectures*. New York: Clarion Books, 1993.

Hoffman, Laura B. "Conversations: Beyond the Shadows of Robert Cormier," Writes of Passage USA, 1996.

Keeley, Jennifer. *Understanding* I Am the Cheese. San Diego, CA: Lucent Books, 2001.

Thomson, Sara L. *Robert Cormier, The Library of Author Biographies*. New York: Rosen Publishing Groups, 2003.

Campbell, Patricia J. *Daring to Disturb the Universe: The Life and Writing of Robert Cormier*. New York: Delacorte Press, 2005.

Campbell, Patricia, J. *Presenting Robert Cormier*. Boston: Twayne Publishers, 1989.

Keeley, Jennifer. *Understanding* I Am the Cheese. San Diego, CA: Lucent Books, 2001.

Thomson, Sarah L. *Robert Cormier*. New York: The Rosen Publishing Company, 2003.

http://scholar.lib.vt.edu/ejournals/ALAN/winter94/Headley.html
[Duel at High Noon: A Replay of Cormier's Works by Kathy Neal Headley]

http://www.achuka.co.uk/special/cormier01.htm
[Robert Cormier: London, July 2000]

http://www.carr.lib.md.us/mae/cormier/cormier.htm
[The Author Corner: Robert Cormier]

http://archives.cnn.com/2000/books/news/11/06/deaths.cormier.ap/
[Robert Cormier, Chocolate War author, dies at 75]

http://www.robertcormier.com/author/results.pperl?authorid=5740
[Robert Cormier: Author Spotlight]

http://www.teenreads.com/authors/au-cormier-robert.asp
[Author Profile: Interview with Robert Cormier]

http://www.webenglishteacher.com/cormier.html
[Web English Teacher: Robert Cormier]

page:

10: Robert Cormier Collection, Amelia V. Gallucci-Cirio Library, Fitchburg State College, Fitchburg, MA.

14: Robert Cormier Collection, Amelia V. Gallucci-Cirio Library, Fitchburg State College, Fitchburg, MA.

20: Robert Cormier Collection, Amelia V. Gallucci-Cirio Library, Fitchburg State College, Fitchburg, MA.

26: Robert Cormier Collection, Amelia V. Gallucci-Cirio Library, Fitchburg State College, Fitchburg, MA.

30: Photofest.

33: Robert Cormier Collection, Amelia V. Gallucci-Cirio Library, Fitchburg State College, Fitchburg, MA.

40: Photofest.

46: © Hulton-Deutsch Collection/CORBIS

52: © Bettmann/CORBIS

60: Robert Cormier Collection, Amelia V. Gallucci-Cirio Library, Fitchburg State College, Fitchburg, MA.

68: Robert Cormier Collection, Amelia V. Gallucci-Cirio Library, Fitchburg State College, Fitchburg, MA.

76: Robert Cormier Collection, Amelia V. Gallucci-Cirio Library, Fitchburg State College, Fitchburg, MA.

Cover: Associated Press, AP

MARGARET O. HYDE, a former teacher, has authored or co-authored ninety books for young people, most about medicine, science, social science, and psychology. She has also written scripts for NBC TV. She lives in Connecticut.